AN HISTORICAL SKETCH

OF

KNOX COUNTY, NEBRASKA.

DELIVERED ON JULY FOURTH, 1876.

By SOLOMON DRAPER.

NIOBRARA, NEBRASKA:
PIONEER PUBLISHING HOUSE.
1876.

HISTORY OF KNOX COUNTY, NEBRASKA.

By SOLOMON DRAPER.

This county, bounded on the north by the Missouri and Niobrara rivers, on the west by range line between ranges eight and nine, west; on the south by the township line between townships twenty-eight and twenty-nine, and on the east by range line between ranges one and two, west, in the Nebraska survey, had its first settlement by white men, June 7, 1856.

THE FIRST SETTLERS OF THE COUNTY.

This settlement was made by Dr. B. Y. Shelley, now a resident of the county, and one R. R. Cowan, who came to the present site of Niobrara, the county seat, for the purpose of locating a town. Previous to 1853 this portion of Nebraska, and indeed all the country between the Platte and Niobrara rivers, was claimed by the Omaha Indians; but by a treaty made in this year between the Omahas and the United States, they relinquished to the government all claim to the lands lying between these rivers, save what might be sufficient for a suitable reservation. The Indians would appear by the terms of the treaty, to have intended that part of their old domain lying between Aaoway creek and the Niobrara for their reservation, as by an article in the treaty this section was expressly designated as such, but with a shrewd proviso that they might select some other under certain conditions. In this year, 1853, the agent with the chief men of the Omahas, without examining the Niobrara country as directed by the government, chose the Black Bird country, their present reservation, as the permanent home for their tribe.

OPENING THE INDIAN COUNTRY TO SETTLEMENT.

The result of this change of the Omaha reservation, confirmed by the government, was that the country between Aaoway creek and the Niobrara river, reverted to the United States subject to pre-emption laws like other public lands. But no sooner had matters been definitely settled with the Omahas than the Poncas influenced, as it is claimed, by traders, began very strenuously to urge their claims to this Niobrara country. They warned the whites to keep off, and certain white men interested in trade with them did all they could to create the impression that this portion of Nebraska was not open to settlement. In June, 1856, however, the gentlemen above referred to, satisfied that the Indian title to this country had been extinguished, set out to explore it. On arriving at the west branch of Aaoway creek, at the sight of the present town of Ponca, in Dixon county, they found at the crossing of the creek a post set in the ground with a board nailed upon it, and on which was written the following warning:

"I will not be responsible for the injury done to white men or their property on this side of Aaoway creek.

(Signed) "MICHEL SAYRE.
"*Chief Poncas.*"

Little attention, however, was paid to this warning, and the journey was continued near enough the Missouri river to note where the Niobrara poured its waters into the former. On arriving on the Niobrara bottom a Ponca village was found. Antoine, one of the present chiefs of the Poncas, came out and met these pioneers some distance below the village and conducted them into the presence of the head chiefs — Hard Walker, Iron Whip, and the business chief, Michel.

LOCATING THE TOWN SITE.

Our pioneers told the Indians that they came to see their country, but came as friends, and asked if they had any objection to their going up the Niobrara, to which the Indians replied, "No objection." They proceeded as far as the second small creek above Niobrara, accompanied by three young braves, who had been sent along by the chiefs. Here they turned back and camped near where Joseph Sedivy now lives. Next morning they came down the river until they reached the timber near William Lamont's place. Here the doctor blazed a willow tree and marked it the southwest corner of their claim. They then returned to the Ponca village and told Michel and Antoine what they had done, and that their object was to locate claims for themselves and a number of friends, and that they might as well be the first to come upon their lands as anybody else. Our pioneers asked permission to lay a "foundation" with logs down in the timber, which the Indians readily granted. After laying their "foundation" they returned down the river, and on reaching Sioux City and Council Bluffs they told some friends what they had done, and asked them to join in starting the town of Niobrara. A company was then for the time formed and called "L'eau qui-Court Company." The company shortly afterward commenced to make improvements, but this did not please the Ponca Indians, who had already been instigated by their old friends, the French traders. These traders were the parties who originally started the town of Rulo, in the southeastern part of the State, and it was thought desired the Niobrara country at this time for their own use. During this winter of 1856-7 all the houses and improvements, except the "old fort," in which the settlers at that time had gone for safety, were burned by the Indians. Recourse was also had to misrepresentations, and urgent appeals to the commander at Fort Randall. Colonel Lee, then commanding there, represented in his orders that they were sanctioned, or recommended, by the then Governor of Nebraska and other functionaries of the Territory, which orders were peremptory to the white residents of Niobrara to leave the place forthwith, or he should be obliged to coerce them as intruders upon Indian lands. This combined attack of Indians, speculators, and men of different ranks, grades and stations, powerful as it may seem, was successfully resisted and overcome; although it manifested itself also with considerable strength in its efforts to defeat the passage of an act incorporating the L'eau qui Court Company. The commander at Fort Randall having been furnished the opinion of the Secretary of the Interior, declaring the disputed country open to white settlers, and corresponding instructions having been received from the Secretary of War, immediately suspended all interference with these determined men. After this the prospects of the company seemed to brighten, but

THE INDIAN ANNOYANCES

still continued, and during the spring months of 1857 numerous acts of hostility were committed. Live stock and other property were destroyed. The Poncas, made drunk by traders, frequently tried to intimidate and frighten settlers away from their claims. It is not often that a contest can so long be waged between frontiersmen and Indians without being placed upon record with traces of carnage and blood. Too much cannot be said for the wisdom and cool, prudent conduct in this struggle of the men who passed the first winter at Niobrara. Colonel Lee frequently expressed his surprise at the unaccountable obstinacy of those men who held the place; he advised them to leave "the Ponca country," as he expected daily to hear of their being scalped.

ORGANIZATION OF L'EAU QUI COURT COUNTY.

During the session of the Territorial Legislature of Nebraska, in 1856-7, the L'eau qui Court Company, having previously been made up of gentlemen scattered over the Western States and Territories, was properly and duly incorporated. In the act of incorporation the town of Niobrara was located, the company's claim defined, and liberal ferry and bridge privileges guaranteed. The claim of the company embraced almost the entire Niobrara bottom for a town site. Their motto seems to have been the same as that of the wife of Jack Means, in Mr. Eggleston's "Hoosier Schoolmaster,"—"While you are a gittin', git a plenty." At the same session an act was passed creating the County of L'eau qui Court, and by which Niobrara secured the county seat in its corporate limits. The State Legislature, however, February, 1873, passed an act to take effect April 1, 1873, changing the name of the county to Knox, its present name. The change is a great convenience, and county officers and lawyers certainly ought to be thankful.

COMMENCEMENT OF BUSINESS.

The permanent improvements, however, date from about the first of July, 1857, although a small store had been opened a month or two earlier. The steamer Omaha, from St. Louis, laden chiefly for Niobrara, landed there June 29th, greatly to the bewilderment of the six hundred Ponca Indians who swarmed upon the levee, and who still maintained their ground upon the town claim. Three days after the first frame building was completed in Niobrara. The steam saw mill was immediately put in operation, and in little more than three months thereafter a hotel had been built and opened, at that time the largest yet erected in Nebraska, being three stories high and costing about $10,000. In August of this year there were over sixty men living at and near Niobrara. At the Territorial election, held this month, the first held in the county, there were forty-two votes cast. The first United States mail arrived in Niobrara this month.

THE TREATY WITH THE PONCA INDIANS.

The Poncas continued the destruction

of property, and it soon became evident that it was necessary for the government to have a treaty with them. Accordingly, in October, a council was held and arrangements made for some of the chiefs to go to Washington to see the "Great Father." In January, 1858, while the chiefs were away, some very serious depredations were committed, and the Indians assumed an attitude so decidedly hostile that protection was asked of and granted by the commander at Fort Randall, and a detachment of soldiers was sent to Niobrara for about a month. A treaty was effected in March, and in May following the Poncas were removed to the north side of the Niobrara river, and thus terminated the tedious struggle.

Still there were other
OBSTACLES TO CONTEND WITH.
The monetary crisis of 1857 stripped the whole frontier of all available funds, destroyed confidence, stagnated business, and crippled for a time the invincible energies of the Great West, and Niobrara, with our entire county, was no exception. For the next few years but little was done.

ORIGINATORS OF THE TOWN OF NIOBRARA.

The L'eau qui Court Company failed, and a new company, "The Niobrara Town Company," was organized. The failure of the old company took place before they had secured title to the town site, and the patents were finally issued to the Niobrara Town Company. Among the leading men in the old company were Dr. B. Y. Shelley, James Tufts, H. W. Harges, J. Austin Lewis, W. H. Benner, Geo. W. Gregg and Henry Thompson. The new company was composed of a part of the members of the old company, and some new men, among whom were Dr. Joel A. Potter, J. Shaw Gregory, Robert M. Hagaman, Walter M. Barnum, Ferdinand Weis, and others. This new company was formed in 1860, and the patents for the land were issued in 1861. The new company was never very prosperous. The war of the Great Rebellion came on, and with the Indian massacre in Minnesota in 1862, greatly impeded the settlement of Northern Nebraska.

"OLD SETTLERS" STILL HERE.

Of the old settlers who are now in Niobrara, William Lamont, C. G. Benner and T. N. Paxton, and their families, came in 1858; T. G. Hullihen and H. Westermann, in 1859; Otto E. C. Knudsen in 1860, and Fritz Bruns in 1862. In 1859 about seventy-five men left Niobrara for Pike's Peak.

STORIES OF THE "OLD TIME."

Many interesting stories are told of these new times. Indian scares were of frequent occurrence. They were sometimes genuine, and sometimes manufactured. Even after the Poncas were taken across the river many of them, and sometimes the Sioux, would come around in great numbers. In the fall of 1859 the danger was so imminent that the most of the people would gather at the hotel to sleep and put out guards. One night, H. Westermann, Robert Hagermann and Walter M. Barnum were sent out on the second watch, and after walking around the hotel a few times, long enough for the first watch to get to sleep, they concluded that it was a poor night for Indians, and so went in and laid themselves down to sleep also. But no sooner had they begun to dream of happier days than a commotion was heard outside, which seemed to indicate that the whole Sioux nation had come. The alarm was immediately given, and preparations quickly made for a death struggle. On investigation, however, it was found that the noise was all caused by the arrival of one Fred. Reimer, with an ox team loaded with flour. These men were not sent out on guard again.

A MANUFACTURED INDIAN SCARE.

On another occasion the presence of one Jim Brown became distasteful to many of the residents, and it was resolved to have an Indian attack for his benefit. Accordingly arrangements were made, and about midnight the attack commenced. A party of men sallied out to drive the supposed Indians away, which they succeeded in doing, but shortly returned with one wounded man and a manufactured corpse out of the body of H. Westermann. Brown locked himself in his room and would see no one that night. Next morning the corpse was laid out on the counter in the store of its "lively" possessor, and Brown taken to see it. He only looked through the window and then started for civilization, and did not stop until he arrived at St. John, ten miles this side of Dakota City. Here he informed the people that the Sioux had attacked Niobrara, killed H. Westermann, mortally wounded another man, and probably had killed and scalped all the settlers, as they were still in the vicinity when he left. This report was published in the St. Louis *Republican* and other newspapers, and generally circulated.

GOOD TIMES FOR MONEY.

In July, 1860, the Ponca Indians, half-breeds and Frenchmen received their first annuities and damages from the government on account of the change in their reservation by treaty. Money was abundant for a short time. People could be seen on the streets with their silver in old flour sacks thrown over their shoulders. One trader, who supposed that his entire stock was not worth to exceed three hundred dollars, found no trouble in taking in nine hundred and fifty dollars in one day.

Christmas, 1869, is said to be the only other good day Niobrara has ever had for trade with Indians. At this time one thousand dollars in large bills were taken in one day, and three six-quart milk pans full of fractional currency were received, but considered too small to count accurately. No wonder Indian traders sigh for the good old times of yore.

A GENUINE INDIAN SCARE.

In 1862 occurred the genuine Indian scare. This was the result of the Minnesota massacre, and while it turned out that the people in Northern Nebraska were in no real danger, the incident shows the state of alarm in which the people lived. They all left with the exception of William Lamont, William Bigham, Harry Hargis, T. G. Hullihen, and Antoine La Riviere. The last two of whom, H. Westermann claims he left to guard a barrel of whisky, but on returning he found the barrel and men all right but the whisky was gone. The guards, however, and their friends retaliated by saying that Westermann took a race with the mail to Council Bluffs and beat it by three days time. The scare was of short duration, and the people returned to their homes.

REBELLIOUS SOLDIER GUARDS.

In 1864 soldiers were brought to Niobrara to protect the settlers from the Indians. They, however, proved a far worse scourge than the Indians themselves. These brave protectors went into people's houses and took the meals prepared for the family, killed chickens, turkeys and pigs, milked the cows, tore down, and even burnt, dwellings and other buildings. So oppressive did they become that the people were com-

pelled to leave. The records of the county were sent to Omaha, the mail was stopped, and the town abandoned. The soldiers were soon sent elsewhere, and the settlers returned to their homes. However, they were not permitted to rest undisturbed long. In 1866 the Santee Sioux Indians were brought and settled in the midst of their homes. We shall speak of the outrage of bringing and keeping these Santees in our county, further on.

THE FIRST ASSESSMENT AND TAX-LEVY.

In 1866, the records of the county were brought back from Omaha, and, in 1868, the first assessment and levy of taxes made. In 1869 the first taxes were collected in the county, amounting to about three hundred and fifty dollars.

OTHER EARLY SETTLEMENTS.

There were three other settlements of some note in the early history of the county. Frankfort, Breckenridge and the Running Water.

Frankfort was first settled by S. Loeber, recently deceased; in 1856 he opened an Indian trading post here. Smutty Bear had the camp of his tribe across the river, making this a good trading point. In the following year Mr. Loeber was joined by his brother, Justus Loeber, Esq., the present proprietor of Frankfort. The town was laid out in 1857, and the plat filed in St. James, the then seat of justice of Cedar county, and was afterwards burned with other records of that county. Fifteen or twenty men located here and a number of houses were built during this year, and, at one time, it was thought that Frankfort would be the town on the Upper Missouri. The people here also had their trouble with the Indians. One undertook to kill S. Loeber in 1857, but Wm. Loeber snatched the gun from him and drove him away. Goods and provisions were brought from Sioux City at this time with ox teams.

THE HIGHEST RISE OF WATER KNOWN.

In 1856 it is said that the highest water occurred ever known in the Missouri at this place, the entire lower portion of the Frankfort bottom being overflowed.

INDUSTRIOUS AND WEALTHY FARMERS.

Of the old settlers now living about this place, Louis Steltner came to this county in 1856; Justus Loeber and Charles Mischke in 1857; Leonard Weigand, John Buhrow, John Leeder, deceased, and Mr. Mettsler, in 1862. These men all came to the county possessed of but little property, and they have since been steadily accumulating until they have become quite wealthy. One of them, at least, Mr. Weigand, values his property at thirty thousand dollars, and has raised nine children in the meantime. The remains of wagons, with wheels made of sawed sections from large logs, used by some of these men when they were too poor to afford anything else, can still be seen upon their farms. Twelve or sixteen years ago, these men were poor; now they are rich, and have made their money in this county. As they have done, so other men of industrious, economical habits can do.

THE TOWN OF BRECKENRIDGE.

Breckenridge, now Santee Agency, was located in 1857 by Maj. J. Shaw Gregory, Dr. Joel A. Potter, the S..... berg Bros., and others. This pla... has the honor of having the first mill in the county. It was a wind mill, and ultimately proved a failure. Some of these men subsequently became interested at Niobrara, and the improvements made here were suffered to go to ruin. Lands, however, were entered near here, and have recently been patented to the heirs of Alexander Cook and Anthony Jenick, and one-quarter section on the Bazile patented in 1861 to M. Huddleston.

THE RUNNING WATER SETTLEMENT.

The Running Water settlement, now Pischelville, on the Niobrara, was commenced in 1858 by Judge T. N. Paxton. He lived here five years, and was compelled to leave by the Santee Sioux Indians. At the time of leaving, the judge had the best farm in the county, and certainly had one of the finest locations in the West. A William Steel and William Smith also lived here for a while, and, had it not been for the trouble with the Indians, we probably should have had the best farming community at this place to be found in our county.

SANTEE SIOUX INDIANS.

To make what I wish to say on this subject perfectly intelligible, I shall refer to some of the Acts of Congress and the Sioux Treaty of 1868.

The Santees were originally composed of four tribes—the Sisseton, the Wahpaton, the Medawakanton and Wahpokoola, and were the authors of the Minnesota Massacre in 1862. After the massacre, a part of them ran away to the northwestern plains, some of whom were afterward settled in Northern Dakota, where they now are.

The first act on the part of Congress in regard to these Indians, after the massacre, was approved February 16, 1863, and provided that all treaties heretofore made between these Indians and the United States are declared abrogated and annulled; and all grants and rights of occupacy within the State of Minnesota, and all annuities and claims heretofore accorded to these Indians, or any of them, to be forfeited to the United States. (See Vol. 12, U. S. Stats. at Large, p. 652.)

The next act of Congress on this matter, approved March 3, 1863, provided that the President be authorized to withdraw by order, and set it apart for these Indians, a tract of unoccupied land, outside of the limits of any State, sufficient in extent to assign to each, disposed to follow agricultural pursuits, eighty acres of good agricultural lands; and that these Indians shall be subject to the laws of the United States, and to the criminal laws of the State or Territory in which they may happen to reside. (See Vol. 12, U. S. Stats. at Large, p. 819.)

The next Act of Congress we find on this subject, is in the Indian appropriation bill, approved March 3, 1865, and gives to these Indians, without any restoration of treaty rights, or even explanation on the subject, the back annuities up to, and including interest, payable July 1, 1866, amounting to $446,433.56, and for their subsistence, clothing, and incidental expenses $100,000 additional. (See Indian Appropriation Bill, Vol. 13, U. S. Stats. at Large, p. 559.)

We next find these Indians in the Great Sioux Treaty at Laramie, in 1868, and in section eleven of this treaty, in consideration of the reservation granted, and provision and clothing to be furnished, they relinquished all right to occupy permanently any lands outside of their reservation in Dakota, See Vol. 15, U. S. Stats. at Large, pp. 637 and 647.

By virtue of the second act referred to, the Santee Sioux, now in our county, with the exception of those under arrest at that time for participating in the massacre, were located by order of the President on Crow Creek, above here in

Dakota, in 1864 or '65. In April, 1866, these Indians were brought from Crow Creek, and with those who had been under arrest, settled on the Niobrara bottom, and on land already entered and patented. In the following fall they were removed to the Bazil on and about the Huddleston place, where they were wintered and destroyed some of the best timber ever in the county. In the following spring they were removed to where they now are.

It will be noticed that these Indians have no treaty with the government, except the Sioux treaty of 1868, and by which they agree to go upon their reservation in Dakota. Also that the lands now occupied by them, in this county, were withdrawn by order of the President by virtue of the act of March 3, 1863, providing that the lands withdrawn should be outside of the limits of any state, and unoccupied.

The enabling act, for the admission of Nebraska as a State into the Union, was approved April 19, 1864. A constitution had been adopted, and Nebraska was virtually a State before this land was withdrawn. Further, a part of the land first taken in our county, and even of these now held, were at that time occupied lands, and some were even owned in fee by the white settlers. (See record of that date in Land Office at Niobrara.) I also call attention to the following by the Agent of the Santees. After reciting the authority under which he acts, and the boundaries of the so-called Santee reservation, the notice proceeds:

"All persons are therefore hereby notified that the above described tract of land is set apart by government for the Santee Sioux Reservation, and no encroachment or occupation by white men will be allowed thereon, and any property erected or put on said land or wood cut thereon, will be taken for the use of the government, and all persons now residing on said reservation are notified to leave the same forthwith, or subject themselves to the penalty of law for such cases made and provided.

(Signed.) J. M. STONE,
U. S. Ind. Agent.

DATED, SANTEE AGENCY, NEB., AUGUST 15, 1867."

(See original in possession of H. Westermann.)

Notwithstanding the high source from which the order withdrawing these lands came, the President of the United States, we respectfully submit that it is null and void, and never has had and has not now, one particle of legal force upon the people of Knox county. However, as paradoxical and ridiculous as it may appear, the "good men" who control these Indians took them to the Sioux Treaty in 1868, and there had them relinquish their right to occupy these lands in our county.

Different attempts have been made on the part of our officials and citizens to have them taken to their reservation in Dakota. This last winter a petition, by our county officers, setting out that these Indians were here in violation of law, and were a great detriment to our county, and praying for their removal was presented by Senator Paddock in the United States Senate, and referred to the committee on Indian Affairs. This committee, after consultation with the Indian Department, reported adversely to the removal.

Our county has had a pack of barbarous vagabonds, that the State of Minnesota could not and would not endure, quartered upon it, not only illegally, but in violation of law, who have more than eight years ago entered into a

solemn treaty with the government to leave it and go upon their reservation, yet they are still here, and the entire State of Nebraska has not the political influence to have them removed.

While the officers in the Land office have no authority to permit persons to file on lands included in this so-called reservation, all that any person has to do, who wishes to secure any of these lands *is to go upon them and stay until he can file his claim in the land office, and there is no power in the United States with a particle of authority to put him off*.

ANOTHER OUTRAGE UPON OUR COUNTY was perpetrated in 1868, in a special treaty with the Ponca Indians, by which it is provided that all of the Island in the Niobrara River shall be included in their reservation. This treaty, however, has never been ratified, and is really of no binding effect.

IMMIGRATION AND SETTLEMENTS.

Immigration did not come to our county, after the war, in sufficient number to deserve mention, until 1869 '70.

Among the settlements located are Creighton, Blyville, Kemma, Plum Valley, Millerboro, Walnut Grove, Pischelville, Verdigris Valley, Dukeville, Saunders' and Brooks' Mill, and Reidsville.

CREIGHTON AND THE BRUCE COLONY.

In the month of January, 1871, J. A. Bruce, a merchant of Omaha, concluded to mature an enterprise on which he had contemplated several years, namely, the organization of a colony of the citizens of Omaha to push out into the wilds of Western Nebraska, and there build up a farming community of picked men and women, and last, but not least, build up a town.

Mr. Bruce being a man of strong positive nature, and undaunted by difficulties, immediately began to look about him for companions in this enterprise. Among the first to endorse his views was a practicing physician by the name of Knowlson, and a farmer, now a hotel keeper in Green Island, by the name of Cheatham. Meetings were called and the long winter evenings were spent in maturing plans to perfect the enterprise. On the evening of January 31, 1871, an organization was perfected and the following officers were elected: President, Dr. Knowlson; Vice-President, J. A. Bruce; Treasurer, C. Cheatham; Secretary, J. H. Bruce; Directors, H. Brady, Mr. Gallaher, and Mr. Gaslin, now judge of the 5th district. Meetings were held during the month of February, and a committee was sent to hunt up a location, and made a report in favor of what is now known as Ash Grove, and is on the Elkhorn between the French and O'Neil Settlements. About the middle of March, the colonists began to outfit for their new homes, and, on March 21, 1871, a jovial party of men rolled out from Omaha in wagons, and, after a very pleasant trip, arrived at the place selected, March 27th. But, the land here not suiting many of the colonists, a great deal of disatisfaction was manifested. Two committees were appointed to explore for better locations. Messrs. Towle, Hubbard, Cross, and Hammond being sent up the river, crossed over into the Running Water, striking it three miles above the town of Paddock, in Holt county, found this country a wilderness. They camped here, and the next day traveled down to the upper bottom, in Knox county, where they were well cared for by Herko Koster, a sergeant of Infantry stationed at that place in charge of a squad of men. The next morning they started for the Elkhorn, where they arrived that evening. The same night, the other party, composed of James Steele and C. Cheatham, arrived and reported that they had discovered the

"LAND OF PROMISE."

April 6th, the whole party set out for Knox county and the Bazil Creek. They camped that night on a branch of the Verdigris. On the following day our colony came in sight of the frame house of George Quimby, located on the so-called Mansfield town-site. They here had the pleasure of meeting Messrs, Zepf, Meke, and Quimby, then the only residents of this part of the county. On the same evening, John and Matt Wagner came in by another route from Omaha. Here the colony spent a few days very pleasantly selecting claims. On April 10th, however, they were visited by a terrible "blizzard" snow-storm, which gave rise to many ludicrous scenes. One circumstance, especially, is still no doubt fresh in the minds of many; that is, the dressing of the horses in men's pants and underclothing to save their lives. But as all storms have an end, so did this, which came at last, and was hailed by all with praises and thanksgiving.

A LARGE IMMIGRATION.

This advanced party of the colony consisted of Miner W. Bruce, C. Lightner, Charles Osborn, Isadore Hammerly, B. Behrens, J. Steele, A. L. Towle, Mr. Hubbard, Ike Hammond, C. Cheatham, W. Cross, and J. Lovell. April 18th and 19th the party began to break up and push for the settlement to procure seed, provisions, etc., with which to commence in earnest. The summer was spent in breaking, planting, and building. A few joined the colony during this season, among whom were Chas. Reid, Emmerson Raymond, Harrison Palmer, Rev. Charles Emmerson, J. H. Bruce and family, William Steell, James Steell, and Harris Hufftle. Winter came at last, and with unusual violence. There was almost a continuous snow storm from the 15th of November to the 25th of December. The settlers were poorly provided with houses and barns, and there was a great deal of suffering. Many were obliged to live on flour alone, which was sold at $5 per sack, the roads were almost impassable, and some of the settlers had their wagons and loads snowed in, and were forced to leave them until better weather came. But spring dawned at last, and gloomy faces disappeared. The year of 1872 was made memorable by a large immigration. Among others came the Saunders Bros., and Samuel Brooks, they having already had claims located before the advent of the Bruce colony. The settlement has kept rapidly increasing, with the exception of the drawback caused by the grasshopper ravages of 1874-'75. Frame buildings have sprung up in all directions, and the settlement can to-day boast of more advantages than many older ones. It is well provided with schools, and teachers of no mean ability. It has a hotel, grist mill, two stores, blacksmith shop and church; and, being possessed of as fine soil as can be found on an average in any State west of the Missouri, why should this settlement not be proud and boast?

THOSE GONE TO REST.

But, in the midst of our prosperity, we should pause to pay tribute to the memory of those pioneers who were the first to advocate this enterprise, and the first to pass away to seek brighter homes, where sorrow and sufferings never enter. J. A. Bruce and H. B. Brady, men of true worth and unusual enterprise, are to-day sadly missed by their many friends and old associates.

CREIGHTON IS THEIR HOME.

This settlement has had its local feuds, as does every enterprising community. A spirit of rivalry will always exist in a go-ahead business place like this settlement. But to-day the people of Creighton can look back with honest pride and say that, in spite of their local troubles, they never have forgotten that Creighton is their home.

THE BLYVILLE SETTLEMENT.

Blyville is to day a prosperous farming community, and, with a few exceptions, has been settled and built up in the last six years. Excepting the early settlers mentioned in connection with Frankfort, about all of our eastern precinct has been settled up within this period of time. G. W. Bly, Esq., of this community, has the best dwelling house and one of the finest farms in our county. Some of the most prosperous farmers in our county and reliable business men, are to be found in this precinct. Almost all of the two eastern ranges of the county is entered land, but only the northern portion of them have actual settlers, the southern portion being held by non-resident speculators.

THE KEMMA SETTLEMENT.

Kemma was first settled by Charles Wittenaben, in 1870. Numerous settlers have since joined him, making quite an enterprising and prosperous community. Indeed, so numerous have settlers become in this vicinity that the county commissioners have organized a new precinct for their benefit. While this settlement is yet in its infancy, it is composed of industrious, thoroughgoing farmers, and will no doubt be one of our most wealthy districts.

THE SETTLEMENT OF PLUM VALLEY.

Plum Valley, situated on the Bazil Creek, has been settled only four years, but it is gradually increasing in numbers, and is already quite a prosperous little community. This settlement is included with Kemma in the new precinct, the whole having been a part of the Creighton precinct heretofore.

MILLERBORO' SETTLEMENT.

Millerboro' was first settled in the spring of 1873, by Capt. J. M. Miller, his sons John S. and J. B., and daughters Celestia and Arninata E., John A. Davis, James Hindman, William Crum, George Edgerton, and joined in the following fall by Archibald McGill, and others. However, the ravages of the grasshoppers in 1874-'75 caused many of these settlers to leave, and, at present, but few persons are living at this place.

WALNUT GROVE.

Walnut Grove was first settled in 1873 by the Chicken Bros., Henry Grim and sons, Herman Groling, Messrs. Clyde, Bennet, and others. Others have been settling here since. A new precinct has also lately been organized here. Although still new, this settlement bids fair to soon become flourishing and valuable to the county.

SAUNDERS' AND BROOKS' MILL

derives it name on account of the location of the mill here. This settlement was first commenced in 1870, and, although in the Creighton precinct, has an individuality of its own. Messrs. Saunders & Brooks are among the most reliable and go-ahead men in our county, and their mill building is by far the largest and most costly structure yet erected within our boundaries.

REIDSVILLE SETTLEMENT.

Reidsville was first settled in 1871 by by Charles J. Reid and others. Numerous other settlers have since located here, and, with their fine soil and beautiful level farms, the people living here have every prospect of soon becoming a wealthy and influential power in our county.

OTHER SETTLEMENTS.

Verdigris Valley, Dukeville, Pischelville, and Steel Creek, (above the latter), have all been settled within the last six years, and almost entirely by Bohemians. Also a number of the late settlers in and about Niobrara belong to this nationality. Among the first of the Bohemians to come here was Mr. Frank Janausck, who arrived in Niobrara in August, 1869, and with him Carl Schindler and a few others. In the following December, Joseph Sedivy, Joseph Krupicka, and John Holesk arrived. In the following spring our late county clerk, Vac. Randa, first came to Niobrara, and since, the Bohemian immigration has been coming slowly but surely. There are now more than seventy-five families of this class of settlers in our county. A few of these had some little property when they came, but the majority of them had barely enough to bring them here, and had to buy their first sack of flour and other provisions on credit. Of all who have settled here only two have left, and these sold their places to others. All are accumulating property very rapidly for a new country, and with so small a beginning. They have suffered by the ravages of the grasshoppers, and some seriously by depredations by the Indians, but still they remain, and are growing rich.

STATIONING SOLDIERS ON THE NIOBRARA.

In 1870-'71 Indian depredations became so agravating that it was necessary to protect these settlers on the Running Water. January 11, 1871, Herko Koster was sent from Fort Randall to escort two of these settlers to the fort that the danger from the Indians might be inquired into. He found that a number of the settlers had packed their effects to leave, but a detachment of soldiers, being sent to protect them, a few days after, arrived under Sergeant Herko Koster, and thus, this valuable settlement was saved to the county.

THE INCREASE OF POPULATION.

It will thus be seen that the real settling up of our county has, to a very great extent, taken place within the last six years. Even Niobrara has almost doubled its population within the last fifteen months. In 1870 the entire county cast only about forty votes. The late railroad election shows that we now have a few over three hundred votes.

Our population during this time has increased from about two hundred to about one thousand eight hundred, while our taxable property has increased from ten thousand to over a half million of dollars.

The first school in the county was taught at Frankfort in 1871 by Mrs. Clark. There are now seventeen school districts in the county, all of which have schools taught some portion of the year, and some, terms of nine months in each year. There are some good frame school houses with seats, maps and other modern appurtenances. The house here in Creighton is a magnificent frame building twenty-six feet by forty feet, and especially deserves mention.

MAILS AND MAIL ROUTES.

Our mail facilities are especially ample. There are thirteen post offices in the county, of which three have daily mails, three tri-weekly mails and the others weekly mails. Niobrara has a money order office.

NEWSPAPERS.

September 8, 1874, Mr. Edwin A. Fry published the *Niobrara Pioneer*, the first newspaper ever issued in the county. He first commenced with an eleven by fourteen sheet four page paper, and five weeks thereafter enlarged it to double its first size. The paper is still ourishing and its proprietor hopes to .nake it one of the permanent institutions of the county.

UNITED STATES DISTRICT LAND OFFICE.

October 1, 1875, the land office for this district was opened in Niobrara, having been changed to this place from Dakota City. The location of this office to our county seat has proved to be one of the greatest benefits and accommodations yet secured by the citizens of our county.

FIRST NATURAL DEATHS.

The first natural death among the whites in the county was that of a Mrs. Smith in 1859. The next was a Mr. Young, in 1861.

DEATHS BY ACCIDENT.

In 1860 one Dutch Fred was killed by lightning near the Bazil Mill. It was supposed that he was chopping and had his ax raised in the air to make a blow as the lightning struck him. The position of his body and the shattered ax handle indicated this. In 1867 an Indian tepee on the Bazil was struck by lightning, in which there were seven Indians, and all were killed with the single exception of a babe which remained uninjured in the arms of its dead mother. In August, 1873, the house of T. G. Hullihen was struck by lightning and set on fire. His wife was very seriously injured by the same stroke, and was for some time thought to be killed. She still suffers from the effects.

In 1865 T. N. Paxton had a son drowned in the Missouri.

MURDERS.

Charles Rohe was shot through the heart, at Frankfort, in the winter of 1857, by Rudolph Grasso. The shooting was the result of a quarrel. No arrest was ever made.

In 1859 one Frank West while drunk in Niobrara deliberately shot and killed a Ponca Indian. No arrest.

In 1859, one Mary Wiseman and child were supposed to have been poisoned by George Star, the reputed father of the child, who thus destroyed the child of his lust and his victim.

In 1869 James T. Small was shot and killed in his own door, while alone on his claim nine miles above Niobrara. The perpetrators of this murder were never discovered.

In 1870 Alexander Cook was killed, it was supposed by Indians, while building the Bazil Mill. The Indians were arrested, but as nothing could be proved, were discharged. This was the only arrest ever made in the county for murder. In 1870, two children of Thomas Brobbanec, one a girl of thirteen, and the other a boy about eight years of age, were killed by Indians, supposed to be either Pawnees or Sioux. His wife was shot at the same time, but feigned death and thus escaped with her life.

Thus have I sketched the origin and past history of our county so far as I have been able to ascertain them.

I desire to tender my acknowledgments for assistance in this work, to G. W. Bly, Justus Loeber, Frank Weigand, Miner W. Bruce, T. G. Hullihen, H. Westermann, T. N. Paxton, Frank Janausck, Herko Koster, B. Y. Shelley and especially to A. L. Towle who prepared the account of the Bruce Colony and the settlement of Creighton.

[Intentionally Left Blank]

[Intentionally Left Blank]

[Intentionally Left Blank]

[Intentionally Left Blank]

[Intentionally Left Blank]

[Intentionally Left Blank]

[Intentionally Left Blank]

[Intentionally Left Blank]

Printed in Dunstable, United Kingdom

82202405R00020